fiery poppies bruising their own throats

POEMS BY
ALLISON BLEVINS
& JOSHUA DAVIS

GLASS LYRE PRESS

Copyright © 2023 Allison Blevins & Joshua Davis
Paperback ISBN: 978-1-941783-99-3

All rights reserved: Except for the purpose of quoting brief passages for review, no part of this book may be reproduced or transmitted in any form or by any means, electronic or mechanical, including photocopying, recording, or by any information storage and retrieval system, without permission in writing from the publisher.

Design & Layout: Steven Asmussen
Cover Art: "Let Her Sleep" ©Kelly Edwards

Glass Lyre Press, LLC
P.O. Box 2693
Glenview, IL 60025
www.GlassLyrePress.com

fiery poppies bruising

their own throats

for all trans folks and all vulnerable bodies, everywhere

Contents

My Mother's Unfinished Canvases: A Triptych … 1
Nude Self-Portrait … 2
Josh, … 3
To our firsts, … 4
"Teach my song to rise to You" … 5
Dear Allison, … 6
Josh, … 7
Eyes in the Backs of our Hands … 8
Argument Who Waits in Our Stairwell … 9
Nude Self-Portrait … 10
An Incomplete List of Everything We've Done with Another Person … 11
"The Fever's Children" … 14
We Send Elizabeth Bishop a Mermaid Postcard … 15
The Lionesses of the Mind Are Dangerous … 16
Josh, … 17
Dear Allison, … 18
Embers: An Acoustic Folk Duo … 19
To Those Who Left, … 20
Do You Ever Miss Kansas? … 21
Talisman against Divorce … 22
Domesticity … 23
Dear Allison, … 24
Josh, … 25
Allison, … 26
Josh, … 27
Allison, … 28
False Coda … 29
Reunion … 30

My Mother's Unfinished Canvases: A Triptych

I.
An octopus cradles: paperclips, a peasant blouse,
one Tarot card, three Camel Lights, a shattered flute,
lavender lotion, black nail polish, a goldfish
in its plastic balloon. The goldfish is unsurprised.

II.
The elder of the two
lacks a face. She tests
her wingspan. The tree,
if it is a tree, recedes into
droplets of smolder.

III.
A blue dot surrounded by cream
and emptiness. Blue waits for a dark-haired child, waits
for morning like a telegram—dashes and dots
carried in a leather and horsehair handbag.

Nude Self-Portrait

i'm not lovely
enough
to act this
demanding

i am crow bones
and cold,
cold fingers
salt your heart
i'll eat you raw

Josh,

I hear your ache from five states away—your fingers poised. I keep forgetting to tell you this sensation moves more like smoke. How it slips through curls, slips around my body—thick but weightless—into lungs to choke and curdle. I keep forgetting to tell you how I can't stop thinking about every person who has watched another person push a child into the world, so many lovers chained together, invisible filament: silver, pulsing.

Each morning I push fingers hard into closed lids, electric orange-blue spidering. I float from my bed. A man sings my name in E minor, key of G. The sound of my name vibrating his throat explains better my meaning.

Last time we spoke, I told you I'd become electric slivers like glass found under a cabinet months after a plate dropped and splintered. His singing is the sound, not of breaking or falling, but of my body trying to bind itself back to whole; the sound of the pieces of me in love and how they ache for the pieces of me abandoned on the ground.

My hair is falling out in clumps. You know the MS, but this feels new. I want to be literal now, but this is also every lover who braided and brushed falling too. Josh, write soon.

To our firsts,

When I unbuttoned your shirt, I was a jewel
thief, a mythmaker smearing red ink—dove's blood—
into flowered margins. When I said, *Finish in my mouth,*
I meant: *Love me. Please love me. I am shattered.*

When I lifted my body to straddle your body, everything
turned blue-red like a car chase siren. In that blurred and soft alarm,
I learned words would always slice with sharper teeth. I put you inside me,
thought about my father's empty shoes like boats docked by our front door.

"Teach my song to rise to You"

Nothing between us will heal if I fall apart—
though I want to wishbone my chest at the blade,

claw ribs and veins and fat, just to watch you stitch me
together slowly, just to feel the sour on your breath touch my lungs,

your tongue thread and needle my skin in brambled loops.

How loved I would be then—rebuilt, wood-cut, shaped and sanded,
humming blood rushing every sluiceway, functional again.

Dear Allison,

I meant to write sooner. If only I could string words between tin cans like the cry owls hang in the night. I could find words to scorch your page.

Do you remember years ago, how after treatment failed, I sacrificed my hair so you would have a child? I wish I had a single word for my certainty, dull silver, gleaming like the small scissors in a hotel sewing kit, that each ringlet cut close to the root was a spiral in the spell. Such arrogance, such glee.

I need a one-word way to catch: "My father went to prison when I was nine. He was only gone a year, but his sentence was much longer." Do you have a thesaurus large enough?

When I watched someone push a child into the world, I felt an envy—colder, smoother than porcelain—then uselessness. How sharply could men adore if they could kneel and bask in the cindery glare of what they cannot do (though my husband did)?

Forests burn. My mother has been dead for four years, and I haven't spread her ashes. The singed trunks, kinless, will never return, whether or not I have known them.

Every time I write *I love you*, I hear *Do what I want when I want it*. No beauty promises an alternative.

Cross-stitched blossoms spread: wine stains, wide as a thumb. Dresses me in wounds. Dress me in slivers.

When we burn, we'll incandesce, I bet.

Josh,

I'm drunk again. *Miscarriage.* Is that what we should call it? I'm not sure how to even think. I keep imagining Sharon Olds and her drops like paint in the toilet. Something like that. You'd know her exact words. You always know. I laugh quietly, smile silently in crowds when it happens. Your quotations. You say, *That's it, right?* As if you are unsure. As if any of us might know better. *Endearing.*

Pills too this time. I mean again. I mean remember how I spent my 20s trying to die. That want flashes still in tight gold strings from my hair like holiday tinsel. That old question, *What if?* Imagine. Imagine it. Here I am a directive. How the world would wake up again. How morning and dishes and sweeping and hanging rugs to dry.

This child would still be dead in my toilet.

A poet friend told me today—*I think I love you.* I feel the same. *I love you too.* But here I am anyway. I want to cage grief in my hands with a swoop and clamp, trap grief glowing in a jar with grass and twigs. I want to wear grief like a dyed electric-blue wig. I want grief to rest gently on my shoulder as wings, ready for the melting. Where am I in the middle of this electric-skimming-cold creped-skin wearing grief? Josh, I want to say I am alone with it, but it is so dramatic. I can't manage the drama of alone.

I meant this letter as an apology. For being in this room again.

Eyes in the Backs of our Hands

We wear them like opals that blink,
like atlas moths, but they stare always.

We call the eyes blue—impatient water—
but really, this is the color of kindness

passing us in the night unseen.
Some things are worse than loss:

how radio static blares from our open
mouths, those nights we never came

though we pressed and pressed our thighs.
Loss is always its own favorite sister.

Argument Who Waits in Our Stairwell

Smaller now, shriveled by age,
she might fit in my hand
if I dared. The argument—hairless

and lumpen—should be swept
down the stairs,
out the door. I might pick up
the unraveled lingering bits

with a small damp cloth.
Much of all love is a burden.

Nude Self-Portrait

Petal-tips, sequined fire,
tawny water. No.

I am two nipples puckered—
eyes of fish—

surgical scars on inner thighs
and backs of ankles.

Five days before my mother died,
we thrashed in our borrowed bed,

tantruming, when the phone rang.
Don't answer.

Shattered foot,
mouthful of wayward teeth.

*Can I touch it? Can I
touch it? How about now?*

AN INCOMPLETE LIST OF EVERYTHING WE'VE DONE WITH ANOTHER PERSON

1.
Arms upturned, I think only of my own face—
lines set into my lips, my brow. My face and body a worry
stone. This is a religious experience in Kansas.

2.
Maybe the spires of the castle pierce a sky
like the underside of a shell. Maybe.
Or maybe this is one more dream—look at me—
in which I have to look you in the face, father,
and remind you how long you've been dead.

3.
My wife and I argue about how to explain adulthood
to our children. Much of every story is impossible
to explain. Facts are like divorce and illness—
unfair as the weep and itch of ivy rashed
on legs and arms like patchwork blankets.

4.
When, after the daily pills, the steps
slide bright as notes clinging close in a chord, we forget—
forget and forget. No amnesia descends
smoother than this one.

A sky full of papercuts hangs over morning.
Believe for an hour the ache won't come back.
Wait like the lover home from the clinic.
Baby. Please, baby. Open the door.
Please open the door.

5.
When my body was a shadowbox, chanting, you brought home flowers
and said, *Isn't this what you wanted? Flowers for no reason.
Even though you don't deserve them?* My body is chanting.

6.
Imagine I am Sharon Olds. People pay
to read about my periods—63 days between this time,
wine-dark and clotted, old blood. Years ago
I woke tangled in a woman's legs to bloody
sheets. We laughed and smoked a joint
after I scrubbed my legs in her bathroom.

7.
Stayed. Over and over—water faced, quaking.
My children hear, learn the lesson
of how to not walk safely away.

8.
You remember me silhouetted, hands
on my waist and a pink rising
as cows mill nearby. Maybe a dog
watches hay unfurl. Sweat and diesel,
cigarette smoke, wet dog and dung.
Who smokes anymore, we both think.
You imagine us shopping for oats
at the menonite store. Babies
on my hip, on the floor, driving tractors.

9.
Her cracked egg head poked out from between
my legs, and you hated her. You had to watch
as they put me back together again.

10.
Laura wrote in a poem *somehow, I've come to believe
everything wants to live.* I never explained to her how she's wrong.

"The Fever's Children"

from Sylvia Townsend Warner's Summer Will Show

The night after my father's body slid into its oven, / not at all like bread, / with none of its promise, // I wanted to make someone pregnant. / I wanted to trammel my father's soul, if he had one, if anyone does / before it could escape. // We're tightening locks, anointing doorways against plague. / I remember the nurse with her butterfly needle. / She stuck me three times. / *Come on, little thingy. Please work.* // Once I stood in a ring of seven-year-olds. / When I said, my dad has AIDS, / they scattered like starlings. // I long to write a line that rises / like a mangrove / out of water, into air unmoving, surrounded by black islands of mosquitoes / as dull light carves letters inside gaps between leaf and leaf shadow. // I long to write the line that slides clean / as the bloody knife you left in the sink, grandma, / cleaner even—sharp as the tip of a Spanish bayonet.

We Send Elizabeth Bishop a Mermaid Postcard

Dear Elizabeth, we're all children
of yours, we girlboys and boygirls.
Object if you like. Pour us another.

Someone has taken a razor
to the shadows of hedgerows.
Sandhill cranes cry out to each other
across parking lots, mournful,
prehistoric and absurd.

Elizabeth, we coil our voices
tighter than Victorian hair ornaments
to ask you:

If I hadn't burned my father's irreplaceable body,
would you have helped us hurl his corpse
over the White House lawn?

The Lionesses of the Mind Are Dangerous

After Ursula Le Guin

Yes, and so are the nettles, rain-green and unobtrusive,
and frogs like a palmful of smashed berries.

Everything in the mind shines with toxins. Everything
in the mind waits—*Can you hear me?*—no noise to ramble
itself to soft.
                Everything in the mind sharpens. Everywhere
in the skin sheathed water-folding-electric lurks elbows and counter
corners and children's plastic figurines. *Can you hear me?*

Yes, and doesn't every animal trap what is beloved in its wet mouth
until the color leaches free, a pearl rubbed clean of shimmer?

The animals of the mind dig and linger, devour us and each other.

Josh,

Now I am laundry, loose string snarls braid socks to jeans. Now I am dinner. Ham and box potatoes. I am inflamed buttons. Broken washer, water wrung from towels with my water shaped hands, and the January crisp-dried terry cloth.

I've fallen again. Fallen to bathroom tile. Vertigo is normal, they say.

I forgot to tell you about the floor and the black that circles inside my eyes. I forget, always, to tell you how my son grows. I'll always remember the gleam of buffed tile the day I discovered I was pregnant with him. Your shorn head. How you were the first person I told. His feet are bigger than mine.

Someday my son will hurt a woman as men do. I want to remind you how you are implicated in this somehow—across the country, not his father, but a man all the same. What happened to the man who touched me at seven? Where is that man from college?

Now I am dishes. Now I am coffee grounds plunged and trapped against the bottom of a brittle glass beaker. Do you remember our trip to Oklahoma? What you told me about love in the car? Balance is affected by input, processing, and output. I can't tell where my feet or legs are moving. I imagine my past lovers are my father's old suit coats sold on consignment, hard gum and lint and a bag of my brother's confiscated pot in a pocket. Imagine them like donated hearts in the chests of strangers.

Dear Allison,

Today is Emily Dickinson's birthday, and although I will never downplay her joy—spiky, man-eating, untameable—I can't think of anything but her pain. Pain creased her knuckles as she kneaded the bread. Pain tinted the ink in the inkwell. Pain spread like chintz, and she stenciled the arabesques with a canny finger. Pain held her hand on the train to Boston and walked like a child behind the linens on the line.

Don't get me wrong. I know she loved, and slept, and sneezed, and got bored, but when I think of the Missouri winter inching across your blankets, I think only of her gashes, of her migraines, and of her: our bonebreaker.

Embers: An Acoustic Folk Duo

In my August dream,
Claire wrote an essay
on Christina Rossetti. Kristeva was there.
Air churned with fire, late summer fire.
Any minute a star or two might dive into the pool.

No matter how we cling and claw,
time shucks off her jelly shoes.

My left foot drags.
A clock presides.
Now's as good a day as any.
The creek bed's dry. Stray moons veer.
My wife, she hammers every nail.

No matter how we cling and claw,
time unzips her maxi dress.

To Those Who Left,

The nights grow wings
(thin, insectile). We still lie
together in dim rooms

that rest in the hollow
of an unkind crescent,
winter past the window

that brought its tatters
and panting. Or we lie
on children's park picnic
tables scrubbed raw of stain
and shine by weather

and our backs and knees.
Or we lie, still, in cars
bent over center consoles
or splayed in backseats

fog-breathed windows
like family car rides
only we didn't trace

our shapes into wet
with fingers and o-shaped
mouths. We remember
every time we yelled,
I only did what I told you I would,

remember every time
you shaved closer, closer, closer,
we've forgotten not a single finger,
        not a single breath.

Do You Ever Miss Kansas?

As a girl, I pressed against our front door to pray out the window. My nightgown thin against my skin. The door always colder than the room. My nipples hard, squished. I prayed for a god made flesh and female like my mother. My mother birthed me in Kansas; the latitude and longitude imprinted by her pushing and pushing. I go back often. But where is home for you? Before the washing, before soap and light, how do you become a body that floats through time like murky pond water?

Talisman against Divorce

Poppies seethe in a ceramic vase, blue-glazed and crackled,
but we—we are the lazy miracle of a Sunday afternoon.

We are a hundred nights spent in our sons' feverish beds.
We are ice sheathed on branches and wires and sheets hot from the wash.

We are that rosary of loose stars, black and pollinated.
We are binoculars trained on female red birds we dare not describe as brown.

We are the folded wet washcloth, the forehead, and the blinding white aura.
We are grainy music, the stained pillowcase, the thousandth *I can't*.

We are growing bellies, pillows for a child's head.
We are the blush of remembering, last night you filled everything.

I still smell you on my face and hands.

Domesticity

Some mornings the house is ready
all together—windows still closed,
our eyelids still heavy, all of us
clean and brushed and scented and full.

The children read on the baby's floor
surrounded by last night's trinkets.
The baby hollers. The children smile.
I'm glad I am alive to see it.

Dear Allison,

I've been sleeping like someone inching toward a rage. No bedroom is dark enough. Moonlight hisses, immaculate, as if dropped into molten iron.

I could be a woman—if I were brave enough not to be beautiful. A mountain backs against a crackling blue daybreak like a teenager shoved into a brick wall.

Every morning I stoop. I shamble sideways to the bathroom. How does anyone bear the mirror? Every morning I remember Marge Piercy because she knows what I have to be—in order to button the cuff, to buckle the brace: *a warrior and a witch.*

What do I miss? Walking miles uncountable, limping, speedy, defiant. (The boys across the street name me *bitch, bitch, bitch.*)

If we were in a field—stalks dry yellow, fiery poppies bruising their own throats—I would scratch the scales from the gown of your old wedding dresses, and you would braid my hair.

Josh,

I told you I'm not writing. Yet you wait and wait and wait. Patient as a blank madlib. Patient as yellow. Patient as your letters calling to me from Ohio, from Florida. Am I meant to save both of us? This sounds like an accusation, and I suppose it is. That is female work. Isn't it? I'm furious. You are not the cause. Yet. Here we are. I want violence—the blood of knuckles on a nose. I've only shot a gun once in my life. I can't do it again. But these long days I like to imagine punching someone. Imagine cheek and jawbone tough and tight under my knuckles. I like to imagine I'm the type of person who could do what needed to be done.

Allison,

Harder and harder these days not to begin with light—brick-broken, ground to powder, bracing, frigid, wet.

When I got your text message, I heard my heart, which had gone elsewhere. I won't say hammer, or pound, or thud or shudder. And I won't excuse either of us from that awful moment with an easy metaphor about a bird, or a bowl of cold fire, or anything carnivorous.

I know this: if it had happened to me, an alien sea would cover my head, shingle by shingle, and I could never escape.

Josh,

I can't discuss it anymore. Who types anymore anyway? I'm not the person I was. Not limp-walk, not drunk, mother who turns on the TV and walks away. Please let go of my words. I'm not here anyway. Imagine me the yellow glow of a bug zapper. Do you know this machine? Even in childhood, that death swarmed my hair. One hung, ominous, from the eave of our house. I remember the night I realized I would die. My first true panic. I've not let go of that beauty since. Like cocaine or cheating on a spelling test, any thing I've done to feel alive.

Allison,

I almost became someone who, like Mary Oliver, would have been able to distinguish the scratch of katydids from the scratch of cicadas. See? There. There's the spot. Whenever my phrasing widens like a wing, I know I'm shielding a wound.

Yesterday, you were bed-bound. I imagine minutes clustering around you or falling through you. I also imagine how wrong my visions must be. The lyricism's crass when beauty is a crutch. When beauty is a crutch.

But the unstrung harp is the one I want to play.

I used to think that living in my body was like spending the night in a ruined house.

I had no idea.

False Coda

If I were a mirror inlaid with garnets like horded
baby teeth, if you were a gold knife intent on paring
tongues from mouths to find that good, cold breath
incapable of noise, if we could cradle our beloveds
in one hundred hankering hands, what hymn
might outlast that gleam, that knife's merciless shimmer,

each breast, each cock, each sharp shoulder and elbow
they warned us not to crave, begged us not to adore?

Reunion

after Denise Levertov

Let's pretend we've come back to the castle—the castle that burned long ago.
Let's pretend the ruins are ours. Let's pretend we were once children here.
Damn. The slice of the sea, the grind of the wind, the bleak cry of bells
(like a shudder of leaves, like a cascade of noon, or one feather that dithers in circles).
Let's pretend two children could love each other and the air from every mouth
singing in every language—worshiping the pull of water from dirt, the deluge
of water returning again and again—might shroud them in the warm breath of home.
Let's pretend this is all we remember. Let's pretend we never belonged.

Acknowledgements

Many thanks to the editors of the following magazines for publishing several of the pieces included here, sometimes in earlier forms:

Common Ground Review: "An Incomplete List of Everything We've Done with Another Person"

Raleigh Review: "The Fever's Children" and "To our firsts,"

The Hunger: "Eyes in the Backs of Our Hands"

ONE ART: a journal of poetry: "We Send Elizabeth Bishop a Mermaid Postcard" and "My Mother's Unfinished Canvases: A Triptych"

TAB: The Journal of Poetry & Poetics: "The Lionesses of the Mind Are Dangerous" and "Talisman Against Divorce"

Tahoma Literary Review: all of our letters were published as "Letters from One Disabled Body to Another Disabled Body"

We would like to thank Laura Lee Washburn, without whom this project could not exist. Thank you Roland Sodowsky, Melissa Fite Johnson, Michelle Hendrixson Miller, Greg Stapp, Julie Ramon, Lori Kate Martin, and Shuly Xóchitl Cawood.

Thank you Kristiane K. Weeks-Rogers, Joan Kwon Glass, Diana Baltag, and the whole Small Harbor family of editors and writers.

Josh is grateful for the love and support of too many poets to name: Kurt Van Wilt, Lucille Clifton, Gary Short, Beth Ann Fennelly, Ann Fisher-Wirth, Annie Finch, Patricia Smith, Jeanie Beaumont, Marilyn Nelson, and Cherise Pollard. Thank you to Kazim Ali, Lissa Kiernan, Mary Craig, Darcy Smith, and Claire Eder. Thank you to my grandmothers: Pat, Lorene, and Sharon. Thank you to Rosie, unsurpassable sister. Thank you to Lynn, who saved me more than once. Thank you to Brad, Jerry, and Teresa, who remain. And thank you most of all to Elliot and Ira.

Allison is grateful for the help and encouragement of so many writers and editors who have shared their time and experience along the way. Thank you to the faculty at PSU and Queens. Thank you to my parents and Allison Carter. Thank you to my beautiful children, Mac, Lainey, and Penn. Taylor, you are, as always, the ground where I land and the air holding me together.

About the Authors

Photo: Germiniani Photography

Allison Blevins (she/her) is a queer disabled writer and the author of *Cataloguing Pain* (YesYes Books, 2023), *Handbook for the Newly Disabled, A Lyric Memoir* (BlazeVox, 2022), and *Slowly/Suddenly* (Vegetarian Alcoholic Press, 2021). She is also the author of the chapbooks *fiery poppies bruising their own throats* (Glass Lyre Press, 2023), *Chorus for the Kill* (Seven Kitchens Press, 2022), *Susurration* (Blue Lyra Press, 2019), *Letters to Joan* (Lithic Press, 2019), and *A Season for Speaking* (Seven Kitchens Press, 2019), part of the Robin Becker Series. Allison is the Founder and Director of Small Harbor Publishing and the Executive Editor at *the museum of americana*. She lives in Minnesota with her spouse and three children. For more information, visit allisonblevins.com.

Joshua Davis (he/him) is the author of *fiery poppies bruising their own throats* (Glass Lyre Press, 2023), *Reversal Spells in Blue and Black* (Seven Kitchens Press, 2022), and *Chorus for the Kill* (Seven Kitchens Press, 2022). He holds an MFA from Stonecoast at the University of Southern Maine, an MFA from the University of Mississippi, and an MA from Pittsburg State University. A former John and Renee Grisham fellow, he offers online workshops and private mentoring at The Poetry Barn. Recent poems have appeared in *One Art, The Hunger, Glass: A Journal of Poetry.* He is a doctoral candidate in Literature at Ohio University, and he teaches high school English near Tampa, Florida.

Glass Lyre Press

exceptional works to replenish the spirit

Glass Lyre Press is an independent literary publisher interested in technically accomplished, stylistically distinct, and original work. Glass Lyre seeks diverse writers that possess a dynamic aesthetic and an ability to emotionally and intellectually engage a wide audience of readers.

Glass Lyre's vision is to connect the world through language and art. We hope to expand the scope of poetry and short fiction for the general reader through exceptionally well-written books, which evoke emotion, provide insight, and resonate with the human spirit.

Poetry Collections
Poetry Chapbooks
Select Short & Flash Fiction
Anthologies

www.GlassLyrePress.com

www.ingramcontent.com/pod-product-compliance
Lightning Source LLC
Chambersburg PA
CBHW030141100526
44592CB00011B/993